CARNIVAL EDGE

CARNIVAL EDGE
NEW & SELECTED POEMS

Katherine Gallagher

Published by Arc Publications
Nanholme Mill, Shaw Wood Road
Todmorden OL14 6DA, UK
www.arcpublications.co.uk

Copyright © Katherine Gallagher, 2010
The author asserts the moral right
to be identified as the author of this work.
Design by Tony Ward
Printed in Great Britain by
Lightning Source

978 1906570 42 2 pbk
978 1906570 43 9 hbk

ACKNOWLEDGEMENTS:

'Seeing the Hand' was published in *The Best Australian Poems 2007* (Black Inc).

Acknowledgements are also due to the Editors of the following magazines and newspapers: in the UK – *Acumen, ARTEMISPoetry, Fourteen, The Interpreter's House, Magma, Poetry News, Poetry Review, Trespass* (UK); in Australia – *The Australian Book Review, Quadrant, Southerly*; in India – *Prosopisia*.

The author is grateful to The Society of Authors (UK) for a Foundation Grant in 2008 towards the completion of this book.

This book is in copyright. Subject to statutory exception and to provision of relevant collective licensing agreements, no reproduction of any part of this book may take place without the written permission of Arc Publications.

The cover painting is by Pierre Vella.

Editor for the UK and Ireland: John W. Clarke

for Bernard

CONTENTS

from THE EYE'S CIRCLE
Shapes within a Pattern / 15

from PASSENGERS TO THE CITY
Song for an Unborn / 21
Firstborn / 22
For Julien at Six Weeks / 23
At the Playground / 24
Distances / 25
The Trapeze-Artist's First Performance / 26
Itinerants / 27
Zelda Fitzgerald Practising Ballet / 28
The Survivor / 29
Maldon, Old Mining Town / 30
Homecoming / 32
Wimmera Windscreen / 33
Leaving / 34
Getting the Electricity On / 35
Woman in a Tableau / 36
Chartres Cathedral / 37
The Long Reach Out of War / 38
Unknown Soldier / 39
Dividing-line / 40
Domestic / 41
Momentums / 42
Passengers to the City 43/
The White Boat / 44
Concerning the Fauna / 45
Night in the Suburbs / 46
Kandinsky Journey / 47
The Magic of Hands / 48
November, Bois de Vincennes / 49
Lost / 50

from FISH-RINGS ON WATER
International / 53
Firstborn / 54
A Girl's Head / 55
Nettie Palmer to Frank Wilmot ('Furnley Maurice') / 56
Eastville, 1939 / 58
Relic / 59
Ghosts / 59
Plane-Journey Momentums / 60
Art Class on Observatory Hill, Sydney / 61
Near Keith, South Australia / 62
Scene on the Loire / 63
To Joe: In Memoriam / 63
Homecoming / 64
Alone on a Beach / 66
First Time / 67
The Affair / 68
Lines for an Ex / 69
Poem for the Executioners / 69
Political Prisoners / 70
After Käthe Kollwitz – 'The Face of War' / 71
Girl teasing Cat with Mouse / 72
Tree Planting at Alexandra Park / 73

from TIGERS ON THE SILK ROAD
1969 / 77
In Memoriam for my Brother / 80
Dancing / 81
Jet Lag / 82
Frost Country / 83
1942 / 85
River Murray Reunion / 86

My Mother's Garden / 88
The Gondola at Santa Maria dei Miracoli, Venice / 89
Poem for a Shallot / 90
Reckoning / 91
The Ash Tree / 92
Thirteen / 93
Knebworth Park / 94
A Visit to the War Memorial, Canberra / 95
Slippage / 97
The Lines on Her Palm / 99
Hunger / 100
Poinsettias / 101

from CIRCUS-APPRENTICE
Entente / 111
Laanecoorie / 112
The Year of the Tree / 114
Hedge / 116
Summer Odyssey / 117
From the Sahel / 119
Winter Hyacinths / 120
Hybrid / 121
Thinking of My Mother on the Anniversary of Her Death / 122
Gwen John swims the Channel / 123
Circus-Apprentice / 124
Keeper / 125
GM Scientist / 126
Tanka for a Hero / 127
Priests / 129
Girl on a Bolting Horse / 130
Nomad / 130

On the Pass from Kathmandu / 131
At Delphi / 132
Love Cinquains / 133
The Lesson / 134
Dancing on the Farm / 135
The Last War / 136
Itinerant / 137
Cloud-eye / 138
After Kandinsky –
    Grey Forms (1922) / 139
    In the Black Square (1923) / 140
    Horizontal (1924) / 140
    Contrasting Sounds (1924) / 141
    Blue Painting (1924) / 142
    Yellow, Red, Blue (1925) / 143
    Balancing (1925) / 144
    Tension in Red (1926) / 144
    Homage to Grohmann (1926) / 145
    Counterweights (1926) / 146
    Points along the Arc (1927) / 147

NEW POEMS
Biodiversity / 151
Seeing the Hand / 152
Take-off / 153
Fledgling / 154
The Dance / 155
La Fleuraison / 156
South Beach / 158
Manifesto / 159
Nostalgia Sonnet / 160
The Wild Colonial Boys / 161

Au Pays de la Somme / 162
Common Grounds / 163
The View / 164
Genealogy / 165
Soundings / 166
Snow-fire / 168

Biographical Note / 169

'A fallen flower
returning to the branch?
But no – a butterfly!'

                        MORITAKE

'Still, he sees all things connected,
the body to the universe,
the same laws governing all:
what makes the planets dance,
the apple fall.'

                        NADYA AISENBERG

from
THE EYE'S CIRCLE (1974)

SHAPES WITHIN A PATTERN

I

the eye as voyager   explorer
   moulding the split-second   touch
   a camera   self-directed   flashed links
   a belonging   expectant   the stage
   set inside the waiting   wind seen restless
   along its voice   eye tracing silences and
   the heart's quickening   the reactor of the present
   identifying mechanism   that marshals
   set place   all colour
   in a saving pattern

II

eye as shadow   refined under the eye-lid
   the closed thought   a prompted tide
   shoring the late sunrise   facing bizarre
   helmeted waves that foam and shrink
   slowed under the heat of distance
   locked in a blue sky   keeper of the illusion
   eye as final liberator   that sees the death
   death in a paid country
                    drying to dust the spent tongue
     the hierarchy unbent

III

remembered the eye that's face to face   the true witness
   with exactness of the moment protracted
   jarring the problem   eye the freed interpreter
   that takes the climate   the crying fall
   without solution   offering nuances unchangeable
   and collective found whim
                  the taking reporter that stays neglected
   that fights unuse   feels under surfaces
   guards against the mind's menace
   of a jammed despair

IV

eye is the ear to silence   broken in the sea's channel
   curves of sound turning
                  the thud of a volcano
                     cracked on its rib of earth
   currents echoing   searching within mind's caves
              simultaneous the links
                  heard in the mystical   escape of
sounds
   crunch from a forest   feet   the slow disappearing
   as ear limits what eye can find
   linked in the mind's charge forever

V

    beyond the reckoning of slaves
        the tussle with blindness   with scenes imagined
    that have a saved reality
          the blind man searching his version
              how beautiful his lover   her hair
                a forest   a tree   the moment that's
                    locked away from him   that he
                       can touch almost but not know complete
                    that he must take on trust
                          wondering what light is like

VI

eye is the gatherer-in of lover's glance
    the look of love   understood without words
    the climb to freedom   steady lines building
    to ultimate bridges
                        of passion turned to silence
   returning depth with memories   expanded to the limits
   of earthbound preoccupation   the sudden
   welcome of touch and caring
        half-forgotten   taken-for-granted accepted
   into known canals of distance

VII

held across the eye's surrender   the
   give-and-take of generations
   where landscapes look the same
   sometimes   light and static dark
   sprayed against cracked walls of distance
                                this the aged's
known blanket   slant in having lived
to face the eye's failure   the figures in memory
they can still bring to mind
the love that the eye calls up

from
PASSENGERS TO THE CITY (1985)

SONG FOR AN UNBORN

Child, curled in the night
I call you, know you
feeling your way against the walls.
You are so used to darkness now –
your blind busy limbs
buffet and push, quickening
as you weigh yourself and float.

In the beginning, I ran through hours
trying to feel you real.
Daily I bargained with you,
was cajoled and soothed
by your moves, winning,
always teaching me. And yesterday
you set yourself on X-ray, vividly
thumb in mouth, head down, a plunderer
looping in the sky.

Half-afraid with new happiness
I scanned that picture,
hunting details – your face, body,
you. Suddenly I knew
your eyes were almost ready
to lift the dark.

FIRSTBORN

For years I dreamt you
my lost child, a face unpromised.
I gathered you in, gambling,
making maps over your head.
You were the beginning of a wish
and when I finally held you,
like some mother-cat I looked you over –
my dozy lone-traveller set down at last.

So much for maps,
I tried to etch you in, little stranger
wrapped like a Japanese doll.

You opened your fish-eyes and stared,
slowly your bunched fists
bracing on air.

FOR JULIEN AT SIX WEEKS

Already
you have taken the world
by your fingertips
small hands closing on
grapes of air,
first fruits that you touch
and hold at arm's length
to choose and choose again.

Soon you will learn
how days are layered with secrets,
how the sun always combs back
its fields of light,
how the wind unveils its colours.

You have all the time you want –
a careful mime
rehearsing routines
as old as the eye.

AT THE PLAYGROUND

The March wind whisks against us:
my son, three, starts the roundabout
refuses to get on himself. Today
he has planned ahead, says it's his turn
to push me, watches me on board
and I'm away. I enjoy being passenger,
store all this for later –
the afternoon's lulled moves,
everywhere spring heady
and he in the foreground
racing his years, reminding me
to take care, hang on.

The ground spins, blurs; he begs it
with each command, checks
I'm not going too fast.
'You can't fall off,' he says
smiling, assured.

I know it, this steady pace
contains us both, days overlap: he will perhaps
never love me more than now.

DISTANCES

I see my mother waving – her unfussed
smiling *au revoir*, alone on her verandah,
a small figure half-covered by shadow.

I hold her wave, see myself sharing it
eightfold, once for each of us – a wave
we have grown into

as she perfected it, voiced it over years
listening for the two who died,
losses she carried into her skin,
her children – the only trophies
she ever wanted.

Now I search her face
contained, real as light,
hear over her words sewn into
the wave, 'There are many kinds of love
and I have lived some of them.'

THE TRAPEZE-ARTIST'S FIRST PERFORMANCE

She has practised the tightrope,
daily spinning her taut body
afloat in territory
she would claim as hers.

Now the audience is waiting,
they bamboozle her with flowers.
The scene is drunk on air –
its nothingness
that she must navigate.

Suddenly her head's a map,
a study in letting go.
Below – the fall, the odds.

She throws her act to the audience –
it carries her to them, their rows
of faces. And it is her sky
they give back,
balancing her with their eyes.

ITINERANTS

Her family remember her from childhood
as the one who travelled brightly
in a big-roomed house,
who always played for time.

For years now I have been following her,
taking on her disguises – globetrotter
bon vivant, tasting in a glasshouse-array.
Sometimes I have wanted to halt, finally settle
but still she lures me on, across each brink.
She is my sister, we live our lives twice over –
times we have seen hemispheres in space
the way a bird might – or finding villages
weft with stories, feeling local again.
Feasts, illuminations, we have taken all
to heart – artefacts, trips out to markets
buying more than we could carry.

I can never quite catch her
nor does she ever let me rest, to shrink quietly
into the hedgehog of my days.
No, there is more, she swears –
her foot a shadow ahead of mine, circling out
saltbush and spinifex before our eyes,
daring me on to the next stage –
to take our lives to pieces,
fossick for new stones.

ZELDA FITZGERALD PRACTISING BALLET

Zelda dances, dances
weaves her implacable dream:
sometimes it drifts
but her eye snares it in,
the pattern that she counts on
to screen her other face –
glittering flapper-doll
harrying the night.

All that fever and sequins
discarded like an empty day,
past the fret of her marriage –
the book-heroine yoke.
Beside her old zany flights
she has sworn now to dance for real,
to make her own name. *It is not too late.*

Hours lag, skein the day –
she loops and dips, dizzy with steps:
there are no crowds lighting, wrapping her in
but with each wild leap, she parcels fury,
strains for a choreography
to reach her self.

THE SURVIVOR
for Anna Akhmatova, 1889-1966

A woman sits in a corner of sun
tracing a poem. Slowly
she is woven into it like the day
as smells of burning
carry her outside.

There, soldiers and jailers
are blocking the street,
books are being burnt –
thousands of words collapsing
in on each other. Suddenly
she sees her own fate:
her fellow-poet is taken
leaving her only silence.

She goes back to continue the poem:
it will go on for twenty years
islanded in her head
and Russia will remember her
as a lover
waiting for the ice-walls to break,
for her hermit's cry
to be carried like fire
from hand to hand.

MALDON, OLD MINING TOWN

A breakdown at six a.m.
and no garage till seven; reminisce
pick at stillness, among the ranks
of bullock-drays and the old diggers
pegged to their shadows –
my great-grandfather who
just missed a mine here,
couldn't go deep enough
to crack the golden rib,
and the others like him
who started and stopped
in the overnight of a few years
until the reef went quiet.

Everything's stage-set for history
and tourists
as the miners pass again
in the early morning chill,
spendthrift with ragged success
and celebrated: the town clinging to a oneness
that was theirs – hood-nosed verandahs
over stone-slab footpaths
with relics of the Then
when six million stirred the Banks.

And you listen, touch their golden-
wheel: it spins in your dream as they
come driving up the street
from an age when they chipped the year
on everything – the '54 Bakery, Dabb's Store,
the Hospital and a line of churches…

Then their voices trail off –
gone like the gold they chased.
And you wait, hold your breath…
　Carry their clip-clops
under glass.

HOMECOMING

The coastline
lies in its lace-edge

its rhythms of itself
continuous, familiarizing

contours of geography – pages
from school-lessons, templates

I am busy unlocking
through hours in a plane

and barriers of light
flashed evenly over trees

grown more vivid with absence,
and birds I magnify

like the magpie, ubiquitous,
sitting within its song

as clouds circle, drift.
Everywhere, we are joined by heat:

I drink it, feel new in it,
ponder its sheet-distance from cold

finding myself like a miner
surfacing, clutching at the sky

the weight of sun suddenly
held on his hands.

WIMMERA WINDSCREEN

A silo
blocking out space ahead
breaks flatness   stretches to the eye's
craving for shape
an upright of the mind on dry horizontals
where trees have been stripped
wheat country
cleaned to the bone
where the mirage
lays its tantalizing sea   blueness
from the sky's plate   glazed
where eye must learn to live
without sculpture
moulded out of the earth's surprises
where silo is focus
signposting   functional
the town's blank sentinel
on a railway thread
with Sculthorpe's *Sun Music*
scratching truer   scraping this
any Sunday in March
with the town asleep
a quartet to be shrieked out
amongst its jargons
ground-wheel
the heaped dust of the backdrop
and the actors enclosed
waiting on the right rain
eye combing an earth
where weather's a way of life

LEAVING

we watched seasons
seep into our skins

saw the seasons fail
fought them

now we find ourselves
packing once more

choosing a direction
the sky weightless

tracks ribboning
before our eyes

the cart piled ready
we scratch final messages

wedge ourselves on board
elbows jarring our sides

suddenly the driver
jerking the reins in

hard
as the load tilts

and crockery
starts to break on itself

GETTING THE ELECTRICITY ON

The farm has changed, face-lifted
since we put away the lamps
or hung them up with lanterns, as antiques.
The house is new-veined, lush.

Getting the current switched through – such
fever, a district-do to celebrate:
'We'll be like the townsfolk now,' we sang.
My mother saw the world transformed
by a washing-machine and fridge.

My father, caught by progress in a skein
that swept about his ears,
tracked voyages round the farm
reassured by the sameness of the stars
and lanterns lighting his mind.

WOMAN IN A TABLEAU
after an incident in the Sahel region reported by a UNICEF official

dust shadows her face

                                                            nightmare

drought

                                                            water polluted

the choice between

                                                            giving her child watery mud

and letting him die

                                                            seeing the choice

over and over

                                                            telling her hands

becoming the choice

                                                            giving the baby poisoned

water

his tongue burning now

                                                            forever against hers

CHARTRES CATHEDRAL

The spires lean
into the air
touch the blue inside
of the sky

lightly
a philosophy

a cathedral
about to lift the world
off its knees

THE LONG REACH OUT OF WAR

They will keep restoring the glass
in broken cathedrals

to carry the eye and the colours
that were shattered

They will keep restoring the stone
in bombed cathedrals

to carry the face and the idea
that were crushed

They will keep carrying the burden
of destroyed cathedrals

even as the ashes blow back

Humanity
keeping faith with itself
even as the ashes blow back

UNKNOWN SOLDIER

We have covered him with real flowers
and taken him from country to country.

It's always the same journey –
people standing in the streets
silently saluting
as we carry him by.

And our hands tremble
under his weight,
our eyes are shocked
by the riddle of tongues
presenting the same paradox
in every country –
the whole human voice as background
shrilled to fever
about keeping the guns at bay.

DIVIDING-LINE

He sits and looks into the space
of the table,
lights a chain of cigarettes
over his head.

His heart is burning
down to his shoes.

It should never have happened,
this battle.

But she's gone…
                He can't believe it,
he can still hear her
on their net of wild stings
gathering her things,
                leaving
wrapping up *the life of her own*
she was always telling him about.

DOMESTIC

He tells me I'm the untidiest
nice woman he's ever lived with.
It's our bad joke – I pluck resolutions,
see garbage floating three floors down
have him doing housework,
say we'll eat out, eat less
eat fast, or just let dishes pile up,
find a stairway of paper-plates
to take us right down to earth.

But I don't leave it there,
race through the apartment
picking up papers, carbons,
the half-made poems disappearing
into paper-clips, folders. Suddenly
it's a tidy hinterland –
the desk bare, no books on the floor,
just that coffee-table
better-housekeeping look.

He smiles approval then
our eyes lock together, we purr,
it's love's dream whirring
till I see my two selves again
shadowing each other, colliding –
the writer watched warily by the
Vermeer girl, head down over her chores.

MOMENTUMS

I have known you for a year
and we've chosen yellow flowers
to sit beside.

Now our picnic's over
and you've taken my picture.
We may as well go back, through more pictures –
see children on a hill move into the skyline
past village-houses suddenly painted by sun.

This is our walk – the partnered graining.

If we argue, you say *Don't,
we're wasting breath.*

Our words must float
flaring, extravagant as flowers.

PASSENGERS TO THE CITY

This morning she is travelling
eyes steeled on her knitting,
while the man next to her
from time to time turns his head,
glances briefly at the fiery wool
then looks away.

He is silent as a guard, and she
never speaks. Are they together, some pair
perfectly joined by silence?
Or are they today's complete strangers?

I'll never know, left simply
to knit them together – characters in a story,
a middle-aged couple on a train
waiting for love's fable to happen to them,
for their old lives to be swept aside,
changed, changed – as she keeps knitting,
bumping him occasionally,
at which he shrugs, turns his head quickly
not like a lover, but content.

THE WHITE BOAT
after a Students' Save Our Environment *Exhibition, 1971*

The child's world
is born on a white boat

but these children have fixed on
dead birds and dead suns,
a *papier-mâché* baby wailing
and paper-trees
littered with old cartons,
cigarette-packs,

everything documented
without magic or mercy:

their multiple-voice shrilling.

It spits in your eye
an anti-revolution
dropping warnings over plugged-up rivers
as a frilly lady smiles papery
out of the crumpled span of her hat

and the last white boat
sticks on a black canal.

CONCERNING THE FAUNA

When I see kangaroos on the screen,
I take in the landscape
in one miraculous jump.

It's the same with koalas –
my stomach lifts,
I start climbing the nearest tree.
                      I'm an old hand now.

Once I saw a famous politician
fill a meeting-hall:
his subject, 'Kangaroos and koalas –
our national identity.'

People listened rapt:
by the end of the evening
we were all either
jumping or climbing.

Finally in the hullaballoo
the police were called –
only the fastest got away.

NIGHT IN THE SUBURBS

A solitary lighted window
floats its blazing square.
Shadows around it jell,
buildings and trees edge closer
to its singular announcement.

Steadfastly
the street stays motionless,
silences gliding.

This is Magritte's hour
sweeping surfaces, teasing
as I wait for some ordinary word
like *sleep*
to write itself cleanly
on the shrill window-face.

KANDINSKY JOURNEY

black and white etc
all the colours
close as birthdays in retrospect

you can join in
become a yellow line
on a red blurred-patch

or a ship skidding down
sea-less

follow the curves
let them take you
over the skyline

when you arrive
at a state of shock
the paradox of colour
will balance you

THE MAGIC OF HANDS

Put your hands into fire

The magic of hands
is rarely celebrated

Test your hands
on the heart's edge

The music of hands
is born in flame

the instinctive touchstone reaching
finally beyond fire
      beyond sign-language

to shore each blending
unique as a leap into light

NOVEMBER, BOIS DE VINCENNES

I listen to autumn's
wild festivity
caught in any leaf
as trees gather colour
and leaves burn to their centres –
bonfires across the earth.

All summer has been winding down
to this: the blaze, a dance,
a requiem for the year's leaves;
a fire subsumed into stillness
guarding an inner music,
a flute-voice echoing
again and again towards newness –
spring's first twist of season,
its sheltering braids of green.

LOST

Our child lost in Kew Gardens –
acres, acres and us peeling back
the unimaginable,
desperate for another chance…

Tourists passed smiling – blossoms, trees
blurred into policemen's radios,
children's cries cutting –
a three-year-old's blind signals.

He had gone, vanished
while we raced the afternoon's
frenetic maze, dread and nausea
jagging our ribs.

An hour's nightmares magnified –
waiting in one place as directed,
with reassurances gathering like balloons,
plummeting to a despair.

Suddenly my mother, stern heart
moored between separations, deaths
and years of loving, stood there
marking time, waiting too.

from
FISH-RINGS ON WATER (1989)

INTERNATIONAL

I take my countries as they come,
fall in beside other travellers
lifting their lives like lightweight
suitcases carried under the heart
– no questions asked.

On this trail I stake my futures,
know that beginnings are old hat
to be recognised like the moon's stare.

I tell myself this is no fool's
paradise, floating on clouds. Here
I ape survival, sing my cagey repertoire
and occasionally see myself dancing
in a space where hemispheres meet.

FIRSTBORN
for J.

Five hours since the cut,
they carry you in – a little grandee
dewy as a bud, black hair combed
perfumed eau de cologne.

I count your fingers,
eye your bunched fists, perfect skin.
A finished work – wrapped white,
your own person.

I missed your first cry –
now you are here separate, defined.
My stomach twists knives
as I try to hold you, skin against skin,

little voyager
in from your cloud.
Quickly I claim you
as I will again and again.

A GIRL'S HEAD
after the poem, 'A Boy's Head' by Miroslav Holub

In it there is a dream
that was started
before she was born,

and there is a globe
with hemispheres
which shall be happy.

There is her own spacecraft,
a chosen dress
and pictures of her friends.

There are shining rings
and a maze of mirrors.

There is a diary
for surprise occasions.

There is a horse springing hooves
across the sky.

There is a sea
that tides and swells
and cannot be mapped.

There is untold hope
in that no equation exactly
fits a head.

NETTIE PALMER TO FRANK WILMOT ('FURNLEY MAURICE')

> *'...we never said Nettie and Vance, we always said Nettie'n'Vance sliding the three words into a single puff of breath...'*
>
> (Arthur Phillips, at a plaque-laying ceremony to honour the Palmers, 25 July, 1985)

There are always the poems
    what sky-splitting poems I would write
        if only
	Vance is
	determined
	is

The time and the leisure escape me
    still there is Vance's writing
        he has won prizes
	taking on
	the country
	a landscape

My prizes have been for criticism
    When do I get time you ask
        after the chores and the children?
	We are
	'the Palmers'
	or 'Nettie'n'Vance'

Vance is taking on the country
    says we are living in a state of barbarism
        and poetry not enough to change it
	'Nettie'n'Vance'
	you say it
	almost one syllable

Its audience too small he says
    we must develop prose and the drama
        an Australian literary tradition
	a way of seeing
	Our lives
	run together

But if only I had the time for writing
    for my poetry
        I would like the time and the leisure
	My life-story
	my own
	but it will never be

to exploit the tiny talent I've got
    to be more than a *hausfrau*
        my poems   a circuit
	told
	except through
	my daughters

Reviews in the *TLS* and *The Bulletin*   and my letters
   I was encouraged   Still
      that was years ago   there were poems

Now the poetry has become   criticism praised
   merely a laugh   a distraction   to be remembered
      to entertain the children   reminding

Nettie Palmer, Australian critic, essayist and poet, b. 1885, d. 1964

EASTVILLE, 1939

That day Uncle Tom was a hero.
Mostly he was unpopular just for
living with us in the old family home –
taking up space, thinking it was his.

Occasionally he and Dad, bush-boxers,
had bloody fist-fights. But I worshipped him,
would tell my sister, 'Tom's my Dad,
Daddy's your Dad'. The grown-ups laughed.

That morning driving home from Mass
we were skylarking on the back seat –
the Dodge door swung… a strip of gravel
and yellow dust, my sister flew out.

Amidst the cries, Tom grabbed her
by one leg. They called it a miracle.

RELIC

It graces the Women's Centre –
an abandoned pushchair, no canvas,
only the frame, four wheels
and a handlebar:
a sculpture for all weathers,
left in the front garden.

Maybe someone with a sense of humour
dumped it here, a reminder.
The baby is missing, long grown.
The mother has also gone
leaving only this shrill shell
once part of herself.

GHOSTS

Sometimes she studies sepia-dark photographs
from the 1940s – her mother
and grandmother doing farm-chores.

Theirs was never the good life
but occasionally she envies them
their slow days.

Were they to catch her up,
she would feel their reproaches rising
over her, like steam on her dark glasses.

PLANE-JOURNEY MOMENTUMS

The danger of travelling is how
it takes you over, caught in
that today-dress you wear
not for frills but for comfort –
in the confines of an air-tunnel
marked by arrows on inflight-maps.

You read, pick up earphones,
settle to a book, tell yourself
that any disasters are swaying outside
this steady balloon
where you balance the day,
maybe humouring your child
who is flying for the first time.

So much for trying to forget
your innate strangeness to this absurd
transitory life you've taken on –
these dizzying heights, circuits of chat,
odd secrets laced with reserve
and everything blended for your newest
neighbour as though you'd been
living side by side for a lifetime.

ART CLASS ON OBSERVATORY HILL, SYDNEY

Here, the sea's bowl –
the harbour with still, white boats
and coloured flags – a Dufy carnival,
lines crisscrossing, the arch of the bridge
against roofs of scattered houses, shops.
It is afternoon, late summer –
how the promise of ships lies lazily
across the myriad bays
reaching as far as eye can see.

The landscape-class, easels set up
have it leisurely before them.
Their canvasses reflect this bluest of light
where the tutor's words float like gulls
wheeling in and out among Moreton Bay figs.

NEAR KEITH, SOUTH AUSTRALIA

I turn off the highway, follow signs
to a mud-brick cottage
tapestried with bearded grass, hollyhocks,
lavender, geraniums, pigface, sage.

My great-grandmother
who smoked a clay-pipe and bore eight children
lived like this, within bowed walls,
a track up to the door.

Today everything's locked, the single window
rations light. I peer in, picture a family
here in two rooms, children taking turns
to move closer to the fire –

throwing on logs to break the frost
while parents hungered for the promised
good year.

SCENE ON THE LOIRE

All around, a lit stillness.
The moon, placed without shadow
leans like a diva
smiling at her reflection
while almost carelessly

the river spreads – a mind
completely at ease except
in one place where undercurrents
break, take over, where
no swimmer would be safe.

TO JOE: IN MEMORIAM

It is November again, Parc de Vincennes,
the trees perfect globes of gold –
paper-trees, leaves stuck in place.
The wind rustles them as we jog past.
Today we'll bring back a branch,
in a few days the leaves will fade.

When we run you say, 'Lift your feet,
lift your feet,' encouraging me
as you encouraged me out of hopeless
love-affairs. I am running after you, brother,
we are sifting gold in a hollow afternoon.

HOMECOMING

Picking out lights over Darwin,
too dark to see
but the pilot mentions it…

People stir, half-waking
as if instinctively
aware of land below

drawing us into its
sweep of colour.
Now an iridescent sunrise

somewhere over Alice,
dawn-changing colours
in a frenzy,

breath arching the windows. Slowly land becomes
dun-squared, grey-green,

an antipodean patchwork:
this was the explorers'
wasteland and their trial –

Sturt's inland sea
still waiting
as the earth drums messages

and the plane drones
through powdery air.
My head tilts into

the storm of arriving –
past distances, faces
that I have assembled

among words, puzzles stretched to
new meanings over lost times
spaces I can't name, never could.

ALONE ON A BEACH

Alone on a beach
in the company of lovers

you watch the afternoon
lift steady as the waves

one especially insistent
hitting rock   changing colour

disappearing   then
coming again

a hot tongue licking stone

FIRST TIME

Being in love helped –
we could have been sewn together
by the night.

Afterwards we lay in warm grass
staring at an inky
quilt of stars.

Indifferent as usual,
the sky didn't melt
as I felt it might

but still we wooed it,
peeled off our old skins –
gave heaven a twist.

THE AFFAIR

He had a way of looking at the clock
when he arrived,

while undressing. She never
looked at the clock,

knew he'd leave
after an hour or two

and his fetish
was a way of letting her understand

he'd be home
as usual, for dinner.

Still, this was safe,
they could go on for years –

wait, phone-call, visit.
Not enough, but it was something.

How little, she realised one day
when he sent her flowers,

remembering her birthday
and she cried.

LINES FOR AN EX

You used to say thousands of people
have died without water
but no one ever died without love.

I got the gist – it hurt like hell.
I longed to prove you wrong
which you were, with your excuses.

Part of me still loves you –
a shade… For love's sake,
I would go without water.

POEM FOR THE EXECUTIONERS

This is a blinding-place.
Only the hangmen see
fixing the knot of shame
upon their chosen tree.

Moments of waiting shrill,
finally echo out
past the creak of startled wood
and a soon-muffled shout.

Slowly the air recoils
on another unheard plea
and light is locked upon
a desolate, marked tree.

POLITICAL PRISONERS
for Nelson Mandela & Bram Fischer

They call from behind
the wires.

It's still the same message
fenced-off

and their truth floats
upwards. You can see it,

a kite held high, suspended
where nothing particular

is happening.
But they keep holding it

before the eyes
of their jailers

and it sails all winds
in a tiny patch of sky.

AFTER KÄTHE KOLLWITZ – 'THE FACE OF WAR'

'The exhibition must mean something, for all the works were extracted from my life.'
Käthe Kollwitz, in a letter, 16 April, 1917

I

Black paint grits under my nails.
Always death, his death
leaping ahead. My son, eighteen,
how I begged him not to go.
I do not know the squalor he died in,
I only know how grief without hope
is waste.

I make hundreds of pictures
without their bringing me
closer to him – it is as though
I have lost the gift
to put my life into the work.

I am caught at forty-nine
fraught forever by what I cannot change.

II

In every house, there is death –
we are mesmerised, submerged.

For two years I have tried
to draw the mother
who takes her dead child in her arms –
I seek my son as I might find *him*
in the work, but nothing comes.

Only the tumult of the search
has dragged me on
to that point where
language has changed,
where I have changed.
I feared his death too much.

GIRL TEASING CAT WITH MOUSE
after the painting by Guisepppe Maria Crespi, 1665-1747

Girl dangles mouse –
its body half-crouched
head turned away, eyes feverish
while the cat stretches
larger-than-life ready to spring.
Its jet-eyes glint, pacing the moment,
impatient with the game.

These are the ingredients of war:
predators, lust, the moment of no return –
all spinning out of control.
And the girl knowing and not caring.

TREE-PLANTING AT ALEXANDRA PARK
for Julien

Five-year-olds plant an oak,
press the roots firm, their gift.
Late-autumn cold chills, distracts
but they fight back
with cheers and hugs
down their conga-line.

They are making a pact
for all the trees of their lives –
chosen forests:
trees they will draw and colour,
fill with birds and flaring-golds
– that they will climb

stand under in the rain
and be hidden by,
that they will keep
to gird rainforests:
mantled, drenched in a lattice
of undergrowth and light.

from
TIGERS ON THE SILK ROAD (2000)

You stick your tongue out cautiously
to get a taste of life:
snow or fire?
They burn the same.

                          MARGARETA EKSTRÖM
                          translated from the Swedish by Eva Claeson

1969

1 – SIGNS

There are the unseen dangers.
You expect my papers to blow all over Asia.
I note your frown, imagine myself lost,
a derelict with no forwarding address.

I'm all set, I say;
we've talked through this before.
You hover about me.
I'm wrapped – a parcel, ready.

There'll be shrines in Kathmandu,
the floating Taj Mahal, tigers maybe.
I'll ride a camel, visit Amritsar,
see Afghanistan's lapis-lazuli mountains
and explore the Silk Road to Istanbul.

I'll trail incense – jasmine, musk
cardamon, saffron
streaming about my head;
feast on tandoori, korma, massala…

I won't be hungering
for love. But I'll expect
to eat your letters whole.

II – India

My bus crawls across India,
the afternoons catch me like sleep –
looking forward, looking back.
I pick through shelves of cloud,
see you everywhere – your face grinning
wryly, slipping through cirrus bands.

Inside the Vishnu shrine
I'm circling your head
homing on your words.
Through this thin-skinned paper,
(as I read, re-read them),
blurring, they mark my fingertips…

Listen to our voices,
yours still insistent
even as it's fading
faster, fast now…

III – Geneva

Though you're a hemisphere away
here you are: close-by –
our conjuring trick of never parting.

All the old stratagems of desire:
so much unfinished loving,
afternoons snatched out of the fire

as if we believed we could remake
what we had lived. That is love's lie.
With distance I have perfected it.

IN MEMORIAM FOR MY BROTHER
for J.

A photograph slipped out of a bag –
I thought, I've got too many,
should edit them.
Then I saw it was you
sitting among rocks at Barbizon
in your blue pullover.

Behind us, Australia beckoned –
a grand water-lily
squat on the Pacific.
Would we ever make it here?

Those days, leaves scattering:
your skidding marriage;
my stalled affair.
We joked about beginnings.

A ladybird, burnt-scarlet,
blazed up your sleeve,
paused, turning back
on its path. You murmured *Hello*
and your eyes followed as it
flew off in dust-dry air.

DANCING

Nothing has dulled my feel for earth,
its stern gravity-pull,
its cushion of dark.

Neighbours in the flat below
hear my feet tapping
while the rest of the house sleeps.
When I dance in daylight, boards creak:
samba, tango, waltz.

I have acres and acres to dance through,
recharging as I go. Sometimes I find a partner
in a shopping-mall or an uncut field,
my party-face sparking till I'm giddy.
I whirl through tiredness changing the beat,
everything spinning – I'm flying at last.

My eyes glisten, past bitterness –
I dance in my sleep.
Whole streets fly by me,
whole streets have started dancing.

JET LAG

I didn't go round the world. It went around me
crossing time zones in my sealed-off balloon,

following inflight-arrows across Europe,
Asia, Australia. Don't ask what day it is –

my body clock ticks in those concertinaed
intervals between borders and continents,

oceans urging them forward.
I can't find sleep. Instead I have birds

crisscrossing the lanes of my head.
They saw my airship slip by and me peering

through a window, setting my watch
by the stars. I'll catch up with this shaky life,

wrap it around me like a quick nap.
Leonardo put such problems on hold

with his *ornithopter*, needing wings
to flap before it could move.

So much for all that sky-gazing,
wanting to get off the ground.

Now I'll just sleep on possibilities.
I'm still thirty thousand feet up,

nudging clouds like a sunset, the day
slipping through my fingers.

FROST COUNTRY

I

The kerosene-lamp flickers yellow.
Listening to the news over dinner
everyone talks at once. My mother's
voice, drumming through our childhoods,
interrupts, 'It's either you
or the wireless.' *Quiet*, before
the babble again. My father gallops
through stories – his childhood here,
the '14 drought, hand-feeding cattle,
putting the Ninety Acre in
for the first time, how
gold diggers turned farmers.

II

Outside, the evening's wide frost
is coming down. In the morning
the paddocks will be whiter
than snow. My fingers
will curl back with cold, beyond
their thrusts for information – sums,
copying my sister, half a column
behind. Later the teacher shows me
how to add up, take-away –
maths with fingers, counting.
Taking in a landscape, I'll soon find
my own way home from school.

III

Eastville – not even on the maps.
My uncle jokes it's the hub
of the universe, with a church
post office and school
set along the Three-Chain Road.
I make plans to paint
each parched acre green,
wave at the few cars that pass
as I walk the two miles
there and home.

1942

They'd hoped he'd be back for Christmas –
the lights shining down on him, the tree
somehow shielding off the horror. A break.
The family hadn't seen him as a soldier,
in his uniform, among harvested paddocks,
the dried stubble that pricked your legs.

Arriving home, he said *Merry Christmas,*
hugged people and slapped them on the back.
Wandered about the place, eyes crinkled
with strain, lines dug
into his forehead. So young, he seemed
to be either laughing or very sad
as though, in between,
there was nothing.

RIVER MURRAY REUNION

I – Picnic

Mottle-barked, gigantic-trunked
red gums overhang
the water, drop shade –
mammoths with
the strength of oceans.

Nearby an old orchard
floats apple and pear blossom –
random confetti
waiting for a bride.

Today's a different celebration.
I hear the midday air
level into the buzz of flies
and a cicada drone. The thick tree-
silence is suddenly broken
by carillon peals from magpies,
Australia's nightingales,
reminding me I'm back.

For months I've imagined,
magnified the scene, peppered it
with anecdotes, have seized
the sky's still azure, felt
how the sun sweeps through me,
how my twin-lives have come
full circle to this…

Wind spikes the tablecloth
with sand, a speedboat skirrs
the river, briefly drowning
our voices and the secrets
not told in letters.

II – Verbatim

This is the bush,
I tell myself
looking for koalas and snakes,
echidnas, a kangaroo at least.
I imitate a kookaburra –
(my party act for foreigners).
The children cheer.

We wait for the kookaburras
to answer –
one long scarf of laughs.
That's supposed to warn
of interlopers.
I smile – an interloper,
but with my best face on.

MY MOTHER'S GARDEN
i.m. C. G.

Banksias, lemon gums, golden wattle: fire-prone
native trees she was afraid of planting close
to the house. And she preferred the softer greens
of the Europeans. Long summer evenings she'd walk
among the fragrances – lavender, jasmine, rose.
Leaning into the plants, talking to them,
pulling off dried leaves, dead-heading blooms.
Another snip? More water?
She'd scoop up canna lilies, dahlias, daisies
that cascaded over her freckled, weatherworn arms.
She saw herself forever in her *Park*.

Now I circle the rowans, golden ash,
flowering cherry; follow lines of lavender
and bougainvillea – exploding purple.
My feet don't tire of this walk
I've come back to for her sake and mine.

The current owners of the house left the gate open –
they may come back, tell me to go. I have my alibi,
talk to my mother through the soles of my feet.

THE GONDOLA AT SANTA MARIA DEI MIRACOLI, VENICE

Take a marriage on water, with gondolier-
boatmen, dressed in white and red satin,
the artefacts of *ricchezze* – it's already
a grand occasion – the boatmen expect
to row the couple to their tower and not turn back.
It 's natural for the wedding-party
to be enveloped by its own *bonomia*, gravitas:
family, friends, the priest's words singing the air.

A vista of marble and roses, *felicità*
candles sweeping the darkness, and guests' faces
illumined as they stand for the couple,
about to pass this first test of their lives together –
to board the gondola on lapping water,
the calm-boat lined with velvet and gardenias:
the sound of churchbells crashing behind them
and the tower, its fiery vane, always ahead.

POEM FOR A SHALLOT

I am fooled.
You insist on the secret of skins –
how perfectly each wraps you.

You compartmentalize,
I don't know how.
I can peel you back to nothing.

I hunt for what isn't there –
layer upon layer –
down to your cagey heart.

When I try to get away
you've snuck into my breath, eyes,
making me cry

into my hands.

RECKONING

Each foot taking us
faster-slow, shadows
before the range
we angled towards it.
Beyond the scattered
settlements, our paths
spanned out.

Soon we hiked by
waterfalls;
our tracks zigzagged
the mountain's furred skin.
This was like work:
the weight and sweat
of the climb
pulling us back
in our push towards
that line
far away enough
to meet the sky.

Stepping over bramble
we urged each other forward,
leaving everything we knew
behind. The mountain
owned us. Our faces
wore together
like two sides of a coin.

THE ASH TREE

The woodman has the tree in his grip.
He talks to its heart: thirty per cent
of the crown must be cut – it will be denser,
go into itself, discover new shoots.

Surgeon, he sits back in the rope-saddle;
ear protectors shield him from the saw's rasp.
Slowly the limbs are looped, excised.

No breeze, nothing disturbs the leaves
but this interloper intent on his task.
Linking himself to the tree,
swinging on up, making notches.

He goes for the highest branches,
pulls ropes tighter, skids about.
The tree is being bargained with.

This is a listed tree. Fifty years back,
it survived fire – scars blacken the trunk.

Today it lays a lean shadow over the lawn.
History crowds in – we cannot see
the heartwood, sapwood, the rings
carrying each year to the outer bark…

The woodman is coming to terms
with the tree. It will outlive him.

THIRTEEN

Smooth in my palm,
it glows like polished cedar;
on the other side – the dull map
of a monk's tonsure:
the first conker.
I always find it for him.

This time he leaves it,
Come on, Mum,
it's only the seed
of a chestnut…

I pick it up, rub it shiny
in my pocket.
There's a tree inside.

KNEBWORTH PARK

A cave of air softens,
hovers over our heads.
We've waited all year for this:
the March lull, the park
almost tourist-free.

Put your ear
to this unsaddled soil,
sound out the mating-calls
of otters, rabbits, voles;
hear horses' hoofbeats
pound nearer-far.

I have made an altar of calm
among these ageing oaks,
lines of stiff-backed trees.

Our walk circles the ancient house,
grounds set off by daffodils.
A five-year-old sings a nursery rhyme,
wanting to pat sheep. Their beady eyes
distract, promising only puzzles.

We call ourselves comfortable explorers,
notice a wine-glass left among the ferns.
A squirrel skids into wintry hiding.
As the light fades, we study
each other's faces
for signs of sun.

A VISIT TO THE WAR MEMORIAL, CANBERRA

We have scratched their names
on the national bronze

cradled them
in a dark photograph

We have collected their medals
ranked them behind glass

carried their relics
through mirages and warnings

We have taken their legends
the words that couldn't halt

the backdrop-massacres
and tainted forests

We have heard dry laughter
breaking their silences

as they kept marching
despite their chagrin

bagging their history
in the tally of requiems

whispering their names
over and over

in halls of recognition
where feet crunch on boards

and conversations
breed silences

SLIPPAGE

I

They have found an answer,
those people talking to their plants.

Tongues rising,
breath following breath.

Through a carbon dioxide veil
plants take in exhalations.

II

In new council-flat blocks
the windows are uniformly small,

rationing the view. It was never
like this on the mountain.

Years of looking at guidebooks,
wanting to camp in the hills.

III

There was no deluge, only equators
that saw the rivers spill over.

The sky might boil, we would
cover our heads, remembering

love, where we had delayed it –
this fate of avoidance.

We wear our hearts on old sleeves,
tamed by the usual risks.

There is still the wash of sun –
another day, the drying summer.

THE LINES ON HER PALM

I've burnt the barn –
an accident, my fault:
my plans awry,
so what?

I'm the farm hand
who talked to herself,
piled up grain
and worked like a man.

The job was never easy
but I liked that feeling
of giving all I had –
my inheritance.

I slept one eye open
on my few possessions:
the canvas suitcase,
my mother's glass bracelet.

What bargains I drove
lumping corn over
that barn's rickety floor!

I swore I'd make
my fortune, head out
the perimeter-gate
to an uncharted terrain.

The wind blows ashes
around me. They settle,
cover the soil.
I see my losses.

Stand up, try to keep
feet steady;
stalk beneath
the sky's shreds.

HUNGER

She is thinking of the last time he touched her –
how he stroked her, said she was losing weight

as if it represented a country they had to get to, as if
the fat could curl back to the bone like years undone.

And she saw they stood between their shadows and the wolf
who howls for them in the night.

POINSETTIAS
for M.

> ...rock salt....
> a cathedral through which light passes,
> crystal of the sea, abandoned
> by the waves.
>   Pablo Neruda, trans. by Robert Bly

I

Daily she chides
her mirror:

who is this woman
staring back

turning the glass around,
twisting its magnifier

seeing a lifetime's portraits
paraded like miniatures –

herself at fifteen in the school-
concert, on her wedding-day,

in the Alexandra Chorus,
at her son's graduation?

She gathers in her few strands
under the blonde-curled wig

studies her pinched skin,
wanting a sign,

a rouge
in her cheeks

an opposite of surrender.
The love of red will save her.

   *

Solo lamps articulate
each starred bush. Leaves become flowers,
flowers become leaves,
fine red stems shedding fire, sunrise-bright.

She sees herself walking through
their thick wall, a cascade of scarlet
at the hospital entrance.

Daily the tread through white-lined leaves,
the bloodless veined maps, red-topped –
their blazes reminders.

When she grows tired, it is right
to look away, forget
the furrowed richness.

Three months have scarred me…
She studies photographs
from last Christmas:

she and her sons
among the prized
dye-bright coal-flowers

that will not be extinguished,
will fall off the stem
and fold in at their own pace.

*

Her visitors trailed messages of fire.
She touched the poinsettias –
Velvet-strong petals, easily bruised.
If only some of their fire could stay for her,
help her sleep. One operation after another.
She followed her charts; read 'Terminal'
(the doctors' notes carelessly
left on her bed) as if she were
strong enough to know the worst –
the tumour's shifts and moods,
as though her body had stopped
in its tracks, to remind her of the
recklessness of cells speeding up.
The word 'Terminal' hammered her.
If only she hadn't read it.

*

The poinsettias stopped flowering,
their fire finally dissolved in air.
She cut the stems back to half their length,
fed them every fortnight
when the new growth began.

Without their red, the painted leaves,
she felt displaced, settled

into a green of hesitations,
willing herself to obey the plants:
Don't overfeed, use tepid water…

She would carry them
or leave a message for her sons
to bring them from the cellar
next Christmas, nearly
a year away now.

*

The call of plants: the yew
making Taxol that enters her veins
with a slow drip, drip,
taking her through the nexus
of these days - the means, as if
health were a luxury, declaring itself
time after time, the Taxol
winding into her cells,
plumping them back to life.

Again, the treatment - *like
flu and a torrid hangover*
– Taxol, an experiment,
her latest miracle-cure
in the wings. If this doesn't work,
they'll try another.
Tamoxifen. Trials, the wait.
Always the play with percentages
and carcinomas haunting
the space that's left to her.

She wills herself well, meditates,
tells her healer and the others
who offer remedies –
teas, leaves, honey –
It is mind over matter…

They're testing another drug –
Will these cures be ready in time?
she whispers, thinking of next
Christmas, her children –
the body that made them
betraying her.

II

I bring her vegetables,
wholegrain flour and eggs.

She jokes about
eating for her tumour.

I can't bear to hear her say
she's begun to know it.

She pats her swollen stomach,
face twisting in a smile –
I have come this far.

More plans: memory boxes
for her sons; her husband

with such hopes
for them, his paintings –
already dead.

Her face, gritty hard.
*I can allow myself
only so much grief…*

　　*

We listen to the *Kyrie*
from Bach's Mass in D.
She tells me
it's her favourite
and the *tour-de-force*
for her next concert.

She turns up the volume –
*I have to sing it
no matter what…*

She hums an aria,
asks me to sing
soprano to her alto.

How can I enter the mood
that carries her along?

*Singing makes me tired
but frees me –*
her voice lifts
flying; drops,

tugged by a weight;
lifts again;
wavering…

*

Across the street
the florist is putting out
cyclamens, irises, hot-house
daffodils flown in.

Christmas is three months
away. *It'll soon be time
for my poinsettias…*

I think of how their wildfire
catches, spreading
around her.

She says she must
have them ready,
flowering on time.

We read her diary, make plans –
a trip to Kew Gardens
if she is well enough.

*You know those doctors' notes,
I never should have read them…*

She offers me bread,
makes several loaves
to give away.

*Nothing's important any more
but this,* she says, playing
her own game against
all odds,

letting the bread's
thiamine and riboflavin
keep her veins.

Under deft fingers:
curves of dough.
Each loaf is cooling
to its own shape.

from
CIRCUS-APPRENTICE (2006)

ENTENTE

It's that time of the morning
when the suburbs are pure, stripped
clean, and the birds are out,
not changing the subject
whatever it is – with sometimes
a rush of song, as one by one
they fit into their feathers.

Just now there's one
who chatters, never stops,
and there's one who listens,
occasionally answers –
an audience of one is enough.

LAANECOORIE

Laanecoorie on the Loddon, with its long Aboriginal name:
Laanecoorie, the strange sound of it, not knowing what it meant.
The Loddon, fringed by stout red gums, with their knotted roots
reaching down into the riverbed, the stones, the mud.

Laanecoorie, the strange sound of it, not knowing what it meant.
The Loddon, my first river, measuring over my head
and reaching down into the riverbed, the stones, the mud –
more interesting than a dam or mere waterhole.

The Loddon, my first river, measuring over my head.
Prickly January: there to see cousins, swim the Loddon –
more interesting than a dam or mere waterhole.
Ted Malone dived and like a troupe of tumblers, we followed.

Prickly January: there to see cousins, swim the Loddon –
always ready to scream ourselves hoarse.
Ted Malone dived and like a troupe of tumblers, we followed.
Childlike, we trusted the river's bulges, its twists,

always ready to scream ourselves hoarse.
Looking back forty years, two brothers and a cousin lost to *Lethe* –
that day, childlike, we trusted the river's bulges, its twists
as magpies, kookaburras and wagtails swooped by.

Looking back forty years, two brothers and a cousin lost to *Lethe* –
that day, we played water polo, raced against each other
while magpies, kookaburras and wagtails swooped by
and we swam full-pelt into the rippling swell.

That day, we played water polo, raced against each other
and our parents watched, faces mottled in eucalyptus shade
as we swam full-pelt into the rippling swell
with never a thought for the futures in waiting,

carrying with us always the mud and the stones and the memory
of Laanecoorie on the Loddon, with its long Aboriginal name;
aware only of the day, the heat of sun, the cool of water –
the Loddon, fringed by stout red gums, with their knotted roots.

THE YEAR OF THE TREE

I carried a tree
through the Underground.

It was hard. At first,
people scarcely noticed me

and the oak I was lugging
along the platforms –

heavier than a suitcase
and difficult to balance.

We threaded through corridors,
changing lines: up and down stairs,

escalators, and for a moment
I imagined everyone on the planet

taking turns
to carry a tree as daily rite.

A few people asked
Why a tree?

I said it was for my own
edification –

a tree always
has something to teach.

*

Sharp gusts
whirred through the corridors

rustling the branches
as I hurried on

past the sweepers
picking up rubbish, scraps of paper.

*Be sure to take the tree
with you*, they said.

*Don't worry, I'm taking it
to my garden,*

the start of a forest.
When people stared,

Relax, I said,
it's a tree, not a gun.

HEDGE

I am in love with its brazenness:
ferocity that opens up the sun. Forsythia,
my first hedge planted with roots pillaged
from a neighbouring tip. I have watched it spread,
flag its statement: a yellow furore, velvet starflowers
to throw in the air, give to passers-by;
hedge-fire, this harvest I revel in, where gold
is traversed by sun and the thicket locks me into birdsong.

I have been waiting for this special rain:
its sudden flux, lemon butter madness,
the flare of it showering over full stems.

Gold in the hand, mesmeric glints
to shelter in: a saffron-walled room *en plein air*,
an alfresco walk through known treasure.

Here is a riot, undeclared: tree-certainty, tree-silence –
each year a new layer as it spreads its yellow further, further…

SUMMER ODYSSEY
Railway Fields, for D. B.

Between Green Lanes and the New River's
four hundred-year-old waterway,
between ghost Victorian railway cottages
and terraces fronting Umfreville Road,
between the past and present's waiting shell,
lies a rectangular patch of woodland
and hedgerow – Railway Fields, broken by grassland
where young foxes frisk in the evenings:

an eco-tone oasis, where city tar
meets woodland, meadow, scrub –
splendid with chalet, pond, lavender
and briar, bees on bramble, cinnabar on tansy,
till you feel blown away to views on the river.

*

Journey in the Fields... Enter from Green Lanes, past the rowan,
up the cobbled path, old railway tracks. A few minutes in –
nettles, brambles and hawthorn on every side – the birds take over:
songthrush, bluetit and robin amongst the convolvulus, blackberries,
painted ladies, large whites: a whole population of butterflies;
trees and grasses seeding. We've waited all year for this: August
sun, the speckled wood on buddleia, brimstone on yellow-wort.

*

Beside the pond, in foaming clusters,
creamy flowers of meadowsweet;
and there's goatsbeard ('Jack-go-to-bed-at-noon'),
bird's-foot trefoil, majoram and reeds.

Frogs sidle out of the water
head for their thicket, find a log
until it's time to scurry back
to lay their spawn, restart the cycle.

FROM THE SAHEL
   for Aicha Ouedraogo, Nadraogo

Aicha, you give us no survival-heroics, no
doom-histories, as your face, sculpture-solid
reaches out from a front-page spread –
you in floral cottons, wide-eyed, poised
beside the thick-leaved neem you have nurtured
from a seedling – carrying water to it weekly,
gliding sure-footed towards it like an Angel of the Desert,
your face shining under a glass-blue sky.

But you have managed to astound the stars:
resolutely starting over as your lifeline for food, fuel
building materials and health cures became waste –
your homelands stripped. You planted fifteen trees here
in Nadraogo, with just the Sahara's dry promises in your eye.

How do you name your miracles? Of the fifteen,
five survived, including your neem now growing
beanstalk-fast in desert, already over twice your height
and reaching into a tongue-dry, drought-filled sky;
twice knocked flat by straying cattle, twice mended by you,
fastening it to a wooden splint with strips of bark.

Aicha, I know little about you, your days in Nadraogo,
your work in the reforestation commune…
How have you rattled the sky, perfected the art of loving trees?
Your fable of neem stalks our century and more.

(After an article by Michael McCarthy, 'A Tree for Christmas', *The Independent*,
23rd December, 2002)

WINTER HYACINTHS

Pink stalwarts come to chase January –
crinkle-mouthed bells cascading my window,
parading prim and upright
awash with scent:
what are you promising,
an end to grey?

Stage-struck, you leave me bracing –
bunched harbingers,
carrying summer on your stalks.

HYBRID

I have swallowed a country,
it sits quietly inside me.
Days go by when I scarcely
realise it is there…

> *I talk to this country,*
> *tell it, You're not forgotten,*
> *nor ever could be.*
> *I depend on you –*
>
> *cornucopia packed close*
> *with daylight moons*
> *and bony coasts,*
> *the dust of eucalyptus*
>
> *on my teeth; mudded rivers*
> *burnished smooth*
> *under the cobalt crystal*
> *of a lucent sky.*

It is my reference-point
for other landscapes
that, after thirty years,
have multiplied my skies.

THINKING OF MY MOTHER ON THE ANNIVERSARY OF HER DEATH

I search her face across a hemisphere,
embark on one more journey:

Will you come?

She's ready with the thermos,
wearing her brown gardening-shoes,
her glasses slipping forward on her nose.

Says she's been planting dahlias
to make a summer show,

a new display for the place
she calls her *Park*.

Over the cloudbank it's candescent,
close. I dare her to keep up with me.

She shuffles answers
to fit my questions. We float,

almost sisters
in the glide of it.

GWEN JOHN SWIMS THE CHANNEL

September 3, 1939. Early evening
and the sea soughs, sways –
a sketchbook washing calm,
its ribs carrying the meticulous rainy births:
portraits from her many lives.

She has always loved the coastline,
come back to it, the waves' fringed-grip:
daily swimming the Channel, testing herself
against its heave and push.
Ahead, Dover's scribbly-white cliffs,
and beyond, the hills of Tenby –
its beach's curve, her childhood's
patch of sand. She has tested this sea's glass

and painted herself into its mirror
like a cloud passing over. She has more
interiors to match and place, place and match
as again she gives herself to the water,
its moody mountains surging,
pacing her – the archetypal swimmer
planing darkness, with the coast
clearing and Paris-Meudon behind her.

CIRCUS-APPRENTICE

I'm learning it all – acrobatics, clowning,
riding bareback and trapeze,
fire from a sleeve: my hand's a wand.

I weave my life round dancing elephants
who spray the air while turning
their backs on the crowd;

lions who never put a foot wrong.
I'm taking their cue, I've seen
what people want.

Prancing ponies teach me steps:
pacing, adroitness, like my fellow-dancers
keeping their spot.

I'm walking the high-wire, making my mark
poised, balanced, don't look away –
you are my gravity's other edge.

KEEPER

You want me to be a lighthouse-keeper? Fine.
I'll set myself up in a spiralled house
with only books and the cat for company.

I'll learn how the sea looks
turned inside out, how bird cries
are thin winding scarves escaping.

I'll handle looking myself in the eye
when I peer down the telescope,
meet silences ragged as runaway clouds.

No one will know how I value
the way the ships' lights radiate,
how I long for their visits.

I'll stay my ground, teach people
to keep their distance,
maybe get to love this sea-life

drop my anchor, forget the city,
its solidity, after the ribbed
slip and slap of sea.

GM SCIENTIST

No mystery
is sure of him

He carries the storm
from one field to another

His genes glow
with intention

He has tremendous tears
glass tears

His merchandise
flashes neon

The flying seed
cannot escape him

Whatever happens
he will dance on rain

His fingertips
trade desire

Bees damn him
into questions

He is stuck
in a spiralling alphabet

TANKA FOR A HERO

Brave Monsieur Pognon
with a quarter of a heart,
his blood running cold;
he eats for the inner man,
can't believe the state he's in.

It's always the same –
his struggle to the clinic
for a transfusion:
the doctors give him hard hope
and the nurses crisp their smiles.

He takes it on the chin,
believes life's today's tipple
as his heart gears up
a season of good whisky
and meshes a young man's fire.

In the Resistance
he marched into the front-line,
wore his cocky cap,
filleting secrets that lost,
sometimes won, the local wars.

When his friends visit,
they rarely talk old battles:
dare devil escapes –
the risks of that other time,
its *do-or-die* calendar.

Monsieur Pognon knows
he has carried his chances,
his blood so thin now,
and he is left hard-memoried…
encircling his life, this death.

PRIESTS

*Be especially polite,
don't be alone with them, never kiss them,*
my grandmother said. It *was* simple,
they were God's chosen.

There they were, prized men
off in a country of their own,
(that problem of their always
having the answers).

Priests were special visitors,
there to bless the house or for
afternoon-tea: occasions for the Royal
Doulton, silver teapot and chocolate cake.

My mother fussed around, finding cake forks,
making sure the cloth was ironed –
always guarded:

that incident when she was seventeen
decorating the church, and Father Shaw
with his onion-spiker tooth
bending to kiss
her freshwater face.

GIRL ON A BOLTING HORSE

The horse's head forward, not surrendering,
the girl vertical in the stirrups

the black sky gathering steel.
Wind slicing the hair from her face,

the dark curve of herself going faster –
the blur of her brothers, standing transfixed;

she, holding her breath, bone-afraid
and flying…

NOMAD

I've served a prickly queen and sold her lapis combs,
staked a chain of problems for my banker and his books,
traded tears with lovers and not thought fast enough,
flipped a flaky coin and stripped its crescent face.

I've built a craggy house and held it up with stilts,
worn my rags to work and made a plushy pile,
saved the tunes of singers to harmonise a name
and raced along the beach to catch the lacquered tide.

I've mulled the pull of planets in a galaxy of sky,
walked behind the rich and bottled their disdain,
tore my heart askew in the dregs of afterthought,
and spread my wings through knots of air to buttonhole a coast.

ON THE PASS FROM KATHMANDU

Rattling through the Himalayas
on the slow mid-morning bus,
travelling further, further from you –
Australia receding, your face receding,
I feel more and more a captive.

Hindu pilgrims chant and pray
to gods who are surely with us
as the vehicle skids, side-slips:
mountains spiral, ravines gape,
cliffs rise to their full height
over fissures too deep to see.

The driver lurches forward, slumps
over the wheel, eyes white
in the rear-view mirror.

I'm scared body-sharp:
my fractured heart, shepherded all the way
from Melbourne, shocks me to sense
as I wait, breathstruck for a miracle;
the bus swerves again, hovers, rights itself
on a handkerchief-sized plateau.

Gasps, cries, crowd the air,
passengers stagger from the bus.
Knees shaking, I bend down, embrace the earth,
thanking those gods.

There's nothing now
               but to go on.

AT DELPHI

Clouded Yellows, Red Admirals, others I cannot name
weaving in and out of bindweed, daisies, buttercups.
They've flown over wide sea-stretches
to reach these wild grasses, tombs and ruins.

I breathe the scented air, feel the sky's silk,
there for the taking. I can almost unknot
my unhappiness, see how its underside
is the impossible love
I've carried all this way
like spare, necessary baggage.

Can I ungrip it, leave it here
for random gods to give one last blessing?
I hear your voice urging me on
to walk through this
steady fire of butterflies.

LOVE CINQUAINS

Taking
my time to dance
in rhythm with your feet,
I notice that our toes at least
are close.

In love
for the first time,
it felt as if the sky
had gathered in all its spaces –
so still.

Cooking
for a lover,
who can bear the challenge?
Best to throw everything in to-
gether.

Making
conversation,
'How was your day today?'
knowing that whatever you say
will bounce.

THE LESSON

Round and round we circled,
his hand steadying my bike –
interrupted by cockerel cries
and a cow bellowing for her calf.
He was forty-five, I eleven.

We'd done so many circuits
I knew the ground by heart,
every rut and puddle, every tuft of grass.
Balance, it's all to do with balance,
he yelled, stopping to catch his breath.

We'd practised now for days.
I worried he'd give up, leave me
to battle alone, but we rattled on;
at forty-five he puffed a bit –
would I wear him to the ground?

Get your bloody balance right.
Maybe I should let you go?
Dad, don't, I screamed, *please don't, Dad.*
Okay, okay, but go easy.
Remember, it's up to you.
This is worse than hell, I thought.

Then as if by magic, just on dusk
I glided forward, swaying right
to left – moved away from him.
Slowly, my girl, he shouted, catching up,
steadying my wobbles again.
I couldn't see his face but I knew
that he was smiling.

DANCING ON THE FARM

I wanted to dance with my father,
dance fast over dirt tracks,
dance full-flight across creeks;
breeze past the watching crows,
surprise every sheep and cow:

jazz-waltz – foxtrot – jive –
to find some *joie-de-vivre*
that seemed to pass him by.

At my first bush dance,
he pulled me to my feet, saved me
from being a wallflower:
his way to say *caring*.

He was master of the slow waltz:
I'd seen his cool toe-balancing,
the grace of it, guiding my mother
into circles of Lehar and Strauss.
But the foxtrot…
Too fast, he shrugged, *I'm past it.*

I didn't believe him, standing there on the edge
of my dream with his face slightly pained –
as if giving bad news
and the gentle side of him spoke:
a look that said he was vulnerable,

my Dad, opened up,
the weight of days holding his feet
to the boards.

THE LAST WAR

There was only one war, and it was finishing
any day soon. Ears keyed to the wireless,
we waited. Then the news: *Japan bombed*,
gigantic clouds curling, skies burnt scarlet –
total destruction…

We've won, we've won, a conga-chant
round the schoolground, beating tins, sticks:
our teacher joining in – flags, jumbled cries –
uncles and cousins coming back. The war over.

Hiroshima, Nagasaki – ghost towns now.
Over two hundred thousand people
ghosts too. We couldn't imagine it.

The bomb entered our conversation,
a stranger who refused to leave.
Only years on did we become aware
of the pit of ash beneath our tongues.

ITINERANT

Polishing my square-toed brogues,
I think about *journey*, that measure
of breaking out of myself
which never leaves me.

I catch each venture like a living thing;
improvised, it cuts free – shoe-inviting,
pressing the day; my heart drums fast, faster.

I tell myself, *Your feet have never
failed you…* Whatever happens,
the journey's always there:
sometimes dark, sometimes clear,
the way – on this road you're wedded
to – a mountain will appear, climbing
suddenly out of a wall of mist.

CLOUD-EYE
i.m. C.G. d. 19.9.87

The sting in a limbering spring day
foreshadows summer. Through her window
roses plait themselves together beside young-
leafed eucalypts as she, too ill to speak,
slowly becomes my eye in the clouds, the gap
I will see through. No one knows me better
than she who circled my first flight.

I've tried to prepare myself, remembering
her cyclopaedic mind, her gift for solutions.
My bird-mother. I reach out, hold her hands.

She slides down into sleep and wakes again
on this final island, where touch is more important
than words. She grimaces, begs for morphine…
Our world divides. We'll fly differently now.

AFTER KANDINSKY
A SEQUENCE:

'When you arrive at a state of shock,
the paradox of colour will balance you.'

Grey Forms – (1922)

Seals: the beach welcomes them,
tucks them into its summits of colour,
deep palettes. Now they gather
their possibilities, unravel old terrains,
rookeries bustled with meetings, reunions –
searching for continuities, fullnesses that
instinctively, they have claimed for aeons.
It is late. They know the oceans have
darkened, that seas are warming,
turning the hours against them.

Long ago, they learned to love colour,
to pull themselves up on it as they
circled the rip and swell of waves,
believing the ocean was theirs.

In the Black Square – (1923)

A rainbow creeps into shape
above a pristine hill, each breakaway field
imposing itself. The rainbow briefly
commandeers the sky, slings moments
to make you draw breath.

Towers point all-ways to new skies,
fields returned to poppies,
buttercups that sleep under the soil,
wanting to reject the plough,
turn morning inside out.

Horizontal – (1924)

Chimneys, spires, half moons, lean over you
holding the idea of settlement together.

It is night and the city has put itself to bed
once more. Those who have survived

are in their shelters.
When you feel the dream slipping,

you are most endangered. Your enemies
and friends know it. If you lose your balance,

reach for the nearest horizontal.
Nothing, you tell yourself, can save you

from the war about to start.

Contrasting Sounds – (1924)

There are no players for the chessboard.
The trees too have gone, leaving a minor banquet:
dull shapes, at angles to each other: Kandinsky's chariot
sweeping left to right – upwards
marking lines to a hushed universe.

Circles rim shades: the drums of colour
summoning your heart. The atmosphere is as calm
as can be imagined: that calm after the shearers
have been through, taking their pickings,
while black-ringed moons pitch shadows,
putting out antennae, snail-like,
for a new slide forward. They hide a residue of faith.

This is 1924, a quarter of the century folding
back on itself. War is the old solution
where the fat death reigns, a bogey
that can't be bought off. Back to the chessboard –
people study the game. Promises, entreaties…

Long-term winners float on their crinkly sea,
navigate a certain tilt, an aftermath,
believing they have everything to play for.

Blue Painting – (1924)

Let the eye investigate blue
and all the arrows focus gravity.

Across the spectrum – cerulean,
prussian, cobalt –

a patchworld of hues
quilts galaxies.

Remember Earth,
the Blue Planet,

how it takes you into backdrops
for a rose, a hyacinth,

the single flowers
multiplied under a clean sky.

Yellow, Red, Blue – (1925)

Watch the animal eyes that whisk corners
faster than an angel breathing passwords
in a mesh of yellow. Cloud-sure, life flags itself on.
Circle after circle is mapped in the mystery
of a line quicker than an arrow, shot from left to right,
the dark corners turned in on themselves,
while the sea advances up the cliffs.

Presently a cat walks tall out of the waves,
eyes open, heading for the fire at the centre,
the red waves fanned, turned crimson,
surrounded by purples that ferry
the jigsaw's spell. Choices multiply,
resonate, form patterns for love-songs
the heart claims again and again.

In the background, dark moons, resilient,
juggle patchwork squares, lines, and curves.
Light bounces off them as finally the perfect blue
you've been waiting for, dips, tumbles
into the still of the storm, among reds, purples,
all shades – this country you keep coming back to,
that walks you home to yourself.

Balancing – (1925)

Sheering into extremes, prime colours that reach back
to childhood – crayons and paints that you flew everywhere,
sometimes colouring inside the lines, sometimes splashing
on a blank slate, allowing sun to be orange, black or green;
waves to be carmine, tipped with blue.

Traffic isn't one way in this quick-eyed adventure between earth
and sky. Moons sit sublime, harness a catalogue of randomness,
signal where to land. To live in the House of Colours
is to spark cadences in the corners of your heart,
everything translated for its verve and flow.

Tension in Red – (1926)

Every secret is a hidden box. You rein it in
and wait. Years on, you've stored laughter
to keep you steady. The sky flares red,
its fires savage the forest.
                                You remember
when the arsonists cried *wolf*
and their calls defeated you.

As the sun climbs, the sky is strummed
like a guitar – string-ladders of sound.
You see the dispute between red and black,
light offered to travellers between moons.

Red stretches, soars, spills,
                    tantalizes…

Homage to Grohmann – (1926)

Grohmann is surrounded, celebrated
and love is a steely-blue cloud
pierced by the traditional arrow
tracing its map of surprise-seas
transporting bounties, spanning years.

The love-arrow knows where it's heading;
it has shelved and garnered
its own magnetic field, leaving gifts
of clouds merged, wrapping in more colours:
sea-green, ice-blue, purple, red, gold.

On this plenteous circuit, travellers learn
Grohmann's song, how he cleared his head
of dark circles, welcomed the spheres,
the healing music that heightens,
resounds, delivers.

Following his compass, the seas flow back,
mirror stars, illuminate spells:
a show that highlights the carnival
as Kandinsky unlocks the colours,
explodes them in harmonies of eye and ear.

Counterweights – (1926)

Colours compete: there is too much black.
Feral birds catch a swinging moon,
balances intersect; finally
there must be a reckoning between
the innocents and their angst. They write
their letter to the dead, cannot know how much
has been paid, how much is owed.

Who is to decide, who to focus
back on balanced moons,
pulled by irascible tides?

Points along the Arc – (1927)

I

In the innumerable windows,
fires are damped down for the night.
Footsteps patter inside the houses
where windows have become faces, alert
to the eye's wide darts. Watchers place themselves
against the glass, stare out; voices from balconies
sing fragilities, placate the next moves.

Tongues grip the air –
love walks here so silently.
Cracks on the pavement make a starting-point;
worn eyebrow sharp, fine-lined but pale, smudged,
driving hot colours to once more make the running,
spurring neighbours to sit up, look inside themselves.

II

The multi-coloured train slides
into the station on noiseless tyres;
parading, it passes on straight lines, curved
to breakaway criss-crossings, returns,
while belief waits to be plucked from the night.

All life is here: the blending, romance,
meetings, finding new strengths, like a flower
waltzing on air – exchanges
as, for a moment or two, people hesitate,
                    balancing.

Let yourself believe – in love, in colour, the way
it directs your eyes, treats you to sharp angles,
throws you unannounced onto each brink.
You hardly know yourself when your feet
touch ground and the colour has remade you.

III

Knights on horseback train
for the joust, alongside madonnas
holding their children and wondering
when the wars will stop.

There are platforms for announcements
regular as the clack of wheels, brakes,
and doors shuffling open. Travellers

drag their baggage behind them,
negotiating corridors
under skies lit by moons
promised aeons ago.

They know the roads home are written
in the languages of colour – measured
against all odds, against the stars.

NEW POEMS

BIODIVERSITY
after *Lobster Telephone*, Salvador Dali

Lobster and telephone have found each other:
the telephone can't eat the lobster
the lobster can't eat the telephone.

The phone's gone kitsch, wearing
an electric-orange hard-hat,
keeping the day on hold.

Sooner or later it had to happen
that some laser-eyed lobster
would shake off one sea and find another –

a stunned, air-shell ocean of voices
listening to *sterlob sterlob*
lobster language

as if for the first time.

SEEING THE HAND

A hand circles a beach, remembering:

people exclaim at its strangeness; children ask
why it's flying alone like this.

The hand is preoccupied with its past –
what it's done, and might have done.

It has seen itself as a Maker
who could lock and unlock doors.

It has known magic, marked out
boundaries, held loved ones.

It was there at the marriage of earth and sky,
saw the world spin in its palm.

When it unwinds from a fist-coil
its rivers unfold, its plains settle

to be read as the Book of Itself
covering dark moments, the flail

of the whip, the trigger-sharp alert, beside
transformations that amaze; spill over.

This hand – the hand that has been raised
in anger and in peace –

invites: *Stop, sit on your hands.*

TAKE-OFF
after a line by Derek Walcott

Have you seen the way the day grows
around you, neither perpendicular
nor horizontal –

open to whims, new currents,
the sky inviting banks of cloud,
stubborn vaults of air?

How it keeps you balancing
like that angel on a pinhead,
your feet facing all ways into the poem!

You follow it, you're the wind, a gale,
path escalating – you're sure
the day has you in its sights.

And you welcome it, ready
to be astonished.

FLEDGLING

In the boat of his head-to-toe
babygro, carrysoft, milk-scented,
he rides the mini-world curve
of himself,

connecting through the warmth
of his silken skin, kitten-closed eyes,
fine hair – cradled
splendidly within reach.

She's every mother come
together: guardian, witch, nurse,
tracking his belonging,
its completeness stretching sky.

Daily she shows him gardens,
valleys of birds calling his name.

THE DANCE

All around, islands of girls waiting
to be asked – cherry pinks, fern-greens, lilacs,

offsetting lines of dark-suits,
half-shy boys: one by one, couples swirling

away, following each other into the sea
of that crowded floor – everything suspended

in the thinning air, the school dancing on its toes,
Exhibition Swing pumped out by an imitation

Victor Sylvester Band, unsmiling, but practised
as a row of puppets,

a whirl of sedate moves under spotlights,
and me, ready to step

out of that loop…

LA FLEURAISON

    1. Orchid

a fervent watcher
set to charm you

vellum to write on
one cool sentence

a drowsy oberon
lulling the year

a classic eye
coding skies

a capricious mood
for whimsy's sake

smooth-tongued suitor
in the chat-game

a global traveller
trading secrets

the cagey face
of fleet tomorrow

a beacon shine
for offshore days

2. MARGUERITES

Leggy performers
reaching from garden hideouts,
full-face the sun, feisty, parading
pincushion centres – terra cotta discs
fringed in white paling.
                        Leaves, sludge-laced,
shadow long stalks lifting a flower head –
                                      sesamied by sun.

3. CHRISTMAS CACTUS

Tropical, they have taken off from the dark,
drawn further from the secret of themselves.

A cavalcade of sisters, faces lifted,
full-splashed in waxy mauves; fringed
heads braced to salute the season.

Girls at a ball, simmering their whispers,
breakaway islands of dancers swirling
their waltz, each held by solo promises to sun.

Uncrowned, they exult in this
annual pageant, mouths pursed – expectant.

Later, over months, they will hone in
on themselves - bargain again with darkness, await
the shadows of pale moons

and suns to explode their dark.

SOUTH BEACH

This is the dangerous time, sky clouding:
lifesavers on the alert, intermittently moving the flags,
shoals of swimmers still keening the fray.

Only a narrow stretch of ocean left now
between the signposts, the spume growing wilder
lifting more boldly – you imagine yourself drawn in,
tugged all ways past the horizon.

Isn't it enough just to be here on this ivory sand
watching breakers curl against clouds darkening, still far out,
spellbound by the limitless, the reach of coast?

Six o'clock now, the show's closing down.
                              A few paragliders swoop in
while children put final touches to their sandcastle.
Soon they'll carry water to the moat.

MANIFESTO

Don't do an all-white bridal garden
    or plant witch's cave
                black tulips, black roses…
Forget the blue garden that's already
    turned the corner of itself from lapis-lazuli,
        ultramarine to teal   and is settled
      happily in its drab bedding.

As summer burns down, be at home
    in a bonfire-salvia setting
            where visitors
  walk among fire, their hearts rising to the red,
    the blood-flowers wreathed
            scarlet, geranium, rose.

Look for new arbours spinning, tossing petals – gardens
    within gardens – freshly-lit islands under trees
        spaces for dancing in ball-gowns and heels
          the mood swept on by mandolins.

Away with amnesties for sober cul-de-sacs:
        make gardens to splendour your brain.
    Just as you trade seasons,
trade gardens. Bring out your gambler,
risk-taker. Surprise yourself.

NOSTALGIA SONNET
after Frank O'Hara

Have you forgotten the zany way we danced
pivoting round corners at breakneck speed
through a sea of Year Tens who stood entranced?.
'Like flying,' you said, me following your lead –
with tousled hair and tapping toes, again
again, each day a new adventure trip –
hunting poetry from Adamson to Zen
and taking our time, just letting it rip.

Sometimes I wonder why we didn't stay
shining up those days – good times and more.
We wanted to travel, get right away,
see the other side, its open door –
not worried much about beating the drum,
believing our best days were yet to come.

THE WILD COLONIAL BOYS

The Carlton spring hung down that night,
acres of fog licking the ground.

How they skipped – shining folk on the move.
up, down, lift, left foot, right, poet-professor
Vincent Buckley leading a non-stop conga,
in and out of rooms, circling wide; up, down,
accordeon music, that same L.P. – *When Irish Eyes
Are Smiling* – *begorra,* a few party girls,
smiling through:
                poetry whirling the boards –

                hours and hours of it
plaited together by wandering souls,
skip your heart out, Buckley shedding reserve
like fairy floss, skipping as if going somewhere
with only hours to spare – laughing, talking,
breaks for drinks;

       antique tunes, folksongs, the music lifting
Mountains of Mourne and *Tara's Halls,* ballads
echoing from floors, ceilings, windows;
feet tapping the sweet and not-so-sweet shreds
of history – and if you stopped to breathe,
others skipping on, always up, down, leaping fire,

constant to the tune of *Eumerella Shore*
and *The Wild Colonial Boy* –
                for the hell of it and more…

AU PAYS DE LA SOMME

Poppies, roses fill the summer air
blazing, blazing through the ink-red day –
quiet fields, once war's bleak thoroughfare.

Shell-shocked voices surge to challenge prayer,
circle makeshift graves, their broken clay –
poppies, roses fill the summer air.

Rustling winds arise, unleash, lay bare
long dead soldiers' dreams of peace some day –
quiet fields, once war's bleak thoroughfare.

*Gun-smoke, fever, stench, hard-eyed despair –
demon moments skirr, shriek death, decay:*
poppies, roses fill the summer air.

Fires and burning taunt all history's care –
bugles echo, flay this blood-soaked way:
quiet fields, once war's grim thoroughfare.

Gravestones lashed by storms mazed everywhere,
loop back scenes that just won't go away…
Poppies, roses fill the summer air,
frame the fields of war's dark thoroughfare

COMMON GROUNDS

They change colour
before your eyes,
shake complacency –
steppe, pampa, savanna.

Ramblers short-cut through
pockets of meadowsweet,
ox-eye daisies, foxgloves
on moor, heath, sward.

Paddock, pasture, lea
shelve the harvest,
court their own silence

tether the seasons, take
the elements on trust,

hold the story of bird, tree.

THE VIEW
i.m. K.

It was February, the harvesting done
and the stubble prickly, yellowed-brown.
He looked out on his paddocks,
the tall gums pencil-shadowing the dam.
The operations had seared his sides –
ridges of scars, *Snakes and Ladders*,
with the strained muscles slowly folding in.
As he said, the omens weren't good.

I remember the air chafing, the odd fly
accompanying his body's shudders that
jolted him day and night, meeting
morphine that gave only brief respite…

Always with his face to the window,
the paddocks and a pulsing sun outside.

GENEALOGY

From my mother, the eyes of a waltzing woman –
corners to be negotiated with care, on tiptoe at times,
tuning in, turning the music up for *Margie* and *After The Ball,*
       invoking pasts of piano, sax and drums.

From father's side, I swerved with the curve of horses
blinked through a long line of trainers, riders, and pacers
who knew their place.
       Horses that could walk *extravagant*
that could canter into the journey, find their own way home.

My parents came together across tables of sheep and wheat,
alive to the dance of growing and harvesting.
She had her garden - it was as if she could always
carry it with her, along with the keys to the family.

SOUNDINGS

Track the garden
        that fields your tiger.

Track your valerian
        dreaming haywire

        and this map
        that colours you in,
        cache-cache offshoots.

Track your mercury,
        its lasered pulses.

Track your tree –
        its bosky spin-offs

        and your pollen –
        its chain of hours,
        daisy-fire.

Track your windmill,
        its shaky cross-bars.

Track your bridge
        (it's weigh-in time)

        and your rain-barrel,
        your precious catchment
        against quick-burn drought.

Track your diviner –
        its special water-butt.

Track your marsh,
　　its wary bunyip.

Track your rain,
　　its downpour grains.

SNOW-FIRE

Everything has slowed
to a hush, cottony wisps settled
into glazed fields – vast surfaces,
luminous, unscuffed – crisp footprints
covered over in minutes.

    I've amassed all this white,
its thoroughness, marked the speed
of the wrapping. Two hours
under the glide of flakes
and the tableau's remade,
whatever the stark terrain
beneath –
                  its unventured piste,
feathered topsoil, a makeover to last
however briefly – tagging
the beauty of the pause.

BIOGRAPHICAL NOTE

KATHERINE GALLAGHER was born in 1935 in Maldon, Victoria, graduated from the University of Melbourne in 1963 and taught in Melbourne for five years before moving to Europe, living first in London and then in Paris for nine years. In 1979 she moved back to London, working as a secondary teacher and after 1990, as a poetry tutor for the Open College of the Arts, Jackson's Lane, Barnet College and Torriano, London. During this time she co-edited Poetry London as well as working extensively with primary school children. She is currently a member of the Editorial Board of Writing in Education.

In 1978, she was awarded a Writer's Fellowship from the Literature Board, Australia Council, and in 1981, she won the Brisbane Warana Poetry Prize. Her book *Passengers to the City* (Hale & Iremonger, Sydney, 1985) was shortlisted for the John Bray National Poetry Award. She also writes children's poetry and many of her children's poems have appeared in anthologies. In 1994, her translation from French of Jean-Jacques Celly's poems, *The Sleepwalker with Eyes of Clay* introduced by Peter Florence, was published by Forest Books, London. In 2000, she was awarded a Royal Literary Fund Award.

From 2002-8, she was Education Officer for Writers Inc and was Writer in Residence at Railway Fields Nature Reserve, Harringay, London, July-October, 2002.

In 2008, she received a London Society of Authors' Foundation Award. Her poems were featured on the A.B.C's POETICA programme, Radio National in June, 2009.

She has read her poetry at festivals and universities in the UK, Australia, Germany, Italy and France and her poems have been translated into French, German, Hebrew, Italian, Romanian and Serbian.

Recent titles in Arc Publications'
POETRY FROM THE UK / IRELAND
include:

SHANTA ACHARYA
Dreams That Spell the Light

LIZ ALMOND
The Shut Drawer
Yelp!

JONATHAN ASSER
Outside The All Stars

DONALD ATKINSON
In Waterlight: Poems New, Selected & Revised

JOANNA BOULTER
Twenty Four Preludes & Fugues on Dmitri Shostakovich

JAMES BYRNE
Blood / Sugar

THOMAS A CLARK
The Path to the Sea

TONY CURTIS
What Darkness Covers
The Well in the Rain

JULIA DARLING
Sudden Collapses in Public Places
Apology for Absence

CHRIS EMERY
Radio Nostalgia

KATHERINE GALLAGHER
Circus-Apprentice

CHRISSIE GITTINS
Armature

RICHARD GWYN
Sad Giraffe Café

MICHAEL HASLAM
The Music Laid Her Songs in Language
A Sinner Saved by Grace
A Cure for Woodness

MICHAEL HULSE
The Secret History

JOEL LANE
Trouble in the Heartland

HERBERT LOMAS
The Vale of Todmorden
A Knack of Living: Collected Poems

PETE MORGAN
August Light

MARY O'DONNELL
The Ark Builders

MICHAEL O'NEILL
Wheel

IAN POPLE
An Occasional Lean-to

PAUL STUBBS
The Icon Maker

SUBHADASSI
peeled

LORNA THORPE
A Ghost in My House

MICHELENE WANDOR
Musica Transalpina
Music of the Prophets

JACKIE WILLS
Fever Tree
Commandments

www.ingramcontent.com/pod-product-compliance
Lightning Source LLC
Chambersburg PA
CBHW020200090426
42734CB00008B/883